MARKS &
SPENCER

Chilli

**A fiery feast of
red-hot recipes**

Linda Doeser

Marks and Spencer p.l.c.
Baker Street, London, W1U 8EP

T21/7688/5313A

www.marksandspencer.com

ISBN: 1-84461-028-4

Printed in China

Produced by the BRIDGEWATER BOOK COMPANY LTD

Photographer: Karen Thomas
Prop Stylist: Karen Thomas
Food Stylist: Valerie Berry

The views expressed in this book are those of the author but they are general views only and readers are urged to consult a relevant and qualified specialist for individual advice in particular situations. Marks and Spencer p.l.c. and Exclusive Editions Limited hereby exclude all liability to the extent permitted by law for any errors or omissions in this book and for any loss, damage or expense (whether direct or indirect) suffered by a third party relying on any information contained in this book.

This book uses both metric and imperial measurements. Follow the same units of measurement throughout; do not mix metric and imperial. All spoon measurements are level: teaspoons are assumed to be 5 ml, and tablespoons are assumed to be 15 ml. Unless otherwise stated, milk is assumed to be full fat, eggs and individual vegetables such as potatoes are medium, and pepper is freshly ground black pepper. The times given are an approximate guide only. Preparation times differ according to the techniques used by different people and the cooking times may also vary from those given. Optional ingredients, variations or serving suggestions have not been included in the calculations.

Recipes using raw or very lightly cooked eggs should be avoided by infants, the elderly, pregnant women, convalescents, and anyone suffering from an illness.

Contents

Introduction

ORIGINALLY FROM MEXICO, *where they are still an important feature of the local cuisine, chillies have been grown throughout the tropics since the 15th century and now star in dishes from the Caribbean, Africa, India, China and South-east Asia, as well as many other countries. They are the hot members of the pepper family and range from relatively mild to mouth-numbingly fiery.*

As a general rule, small, pointed chillies tend to be hotter than rounder varieties and red chillies tend to be milder than green ones. Most of the heat is concentrated in the membranes surrounding the seeds, so deseeding before use produces a milder flavour. If you have sensitive skin, be sure to wear rubber gloves when handling chillies and always avoid touching your lips, nose and eyes until you have washed your hands.

There are several hundred varieties of chillies, and nearly 200 are grown in Mexico alone. Among the most popular medium to hot chillies are jalapeño, serrano, Fresno, bird's eye, Scotch bonnet, rocotillo, poblano and, hottest of all, habanero. Milder chillies range from the sweet flavoured Anaheim and cherry varieties to banana and chilaca chillies.

Chillies may be pickled or smoked, and jalapeño is a favourite for both of these treatments. Dried chillies such as ancho, the dried version of poblano, are an invaluable store cupboard stand-by because they can be soaked in warm water to reconstitute them or they can simply be crumbled.

Whether you enjoy the thrill of a flaming-hot mouth or you prefer the more subtle side of this colourful ingredient, cooking with chillies can lend spice to your dining table all year round.

Chillies Rellenos

3 eggs, separated

55 g/2 oz plain flour

325 g/11¹/₂ oz Cheddar or other
semi-hard cheese

16 fresh jalapeño chillies

sunflower or corn oil, for deep-frying

These spicy Mexican mouthfuls make a great appetizer or are delicious served with pre-dinner drinks.

1 Whisk the egg whites in a dry, grease-free bowl until stiff. Beat the egg yolks in a separate bowl, then fold in the whites. Spread out the flour in a shallow dish. Cut 225 g/8 oz of the cheese into 16 sticks and grate the remainder.

2 Make a slit in the side of each chilli and scrape out the seeds. Rinse the cavities and pat dry with kitchen paper. Place a stick of cheese inside each chilli.

3 Preheat the grill. Heat the oil for deep-frying to 180–190°C/ 350–375°F, or until a cube of bread dropped into the oil browns in 30 seconds. Dip the chillies into the egg mixture, then into the flour. Deep-fry, turning occasionally, until golden brown all over. Drain well on kitchen paper.

4 Arrange the chillies in a flameproof dish and sprinkle over the grated cheese. Place under the grill until the cheese has melted, then serve.

Guacamole

SERVES 4

PREPARATION TIME: 15 MINUTES

COOKING TIME: NONE

2 avocados

1 fresh green chilli, deseeded and finely chopped

2 fresh red chillies, deseeded and finely chopped

1 garlic clove, finely chopped

4 spring onions, finely chopped

2 tbsp olive oil, plus extra for drizzling

juice of 1 lime

salt

fresh coriander leaves, to garnish

tortilla chips, to serve

You can also serve this fiery dip with raw vegetable sticks or spoon it over grilled steak or chops.

1 Halve the avocados and remove the stones. Using a spoon, scoop the flesh into a bowl and mash with a fork to a soft, chunky consistency.

2 Stir the chillies, garlic, spring onions, olive oil and lime juice into the mashed avocado and season to taste with salt. If you prefer a smooth dip, place the avocado flesh, chillies, garlic, spring onions, oil and lime juice in a food processor or blender and process to a purée.

3 Spoon the guacamole into a serving bowl and drizzle a little extra olive oil over the top. Sprinkle with coriander leaves.

4 If you are not serving the guacamole immediately, cover the bowl tightly with clingfilm to prevent discolouration and store in the refrigerator for no longer than 2 hours. Serve with tortilla chips.

Spring Rolls with
Sweet Chilli Dipping Sauce

These spicy Thai favourites make a wonderful first course and unusual party food.

1 For the sauce, heat the vinegar, water and sugar in a saucepan, stirring to dissolve the sugar. Bring to the boil and boil, without stirring, until syrupy. Stir in the chillies and reserve. Meanwhile, soak the noodles according to the packet instructions. Drain, then cut into short lengths.

2 Heat 2 tablespoons oil in a preheated wok. Add the chillies and garlic and stir-fry for 1 minute. Add the pork and stir-fry for 2 minutes, until browned. Add the Chinese leaves, carrot, noodles, sugar, fish and oyster sauces and stir-fry for 3 minutes. Cool.

3 Place 2 teaspoons of filling on each wrapper and roll up, tucking in the sides. Brush the edge with egg white. Heat the oil for deep-frying to 180–190°C/ 350–375°F, or until a cube of bread browns in 30 seconds. Deep-fry the rolls for 3 minutes, until golden. Drain and serve with the sauce.

MAKES 20 ROLLS

PREPARATION TIME: 30 MINUTES, PLUS 30 MINUTES COOLING
COOKING TIME: 20–25 MINUTES

85 g/3 oz cellophane noodles

2 tbsp groundnut or sunflower oil, plus extra for deep-frying

1–2 fresh bird's eye chillies, deseeded and chopped

2 garlic cloves, finely chopped

225 g/8 oz fresh pork mince

85 g/3 oz Chinese leaves, finely shredded

1 carrot, cut into thin batons

1 tbsp sugar

2 tbsp Thai fish sauce

2 tbsp oyster sauce

20 spring roll wrappers, thawed if frozen

1 egg white, lightly beaten

For the dipping sauce

4 tbsp rice vinegar

2 tbsp water

55 g/2 oz caster sugar

2 fresh bird's eye chillies, deseeded and finely chopped

Middle Eastern Soup with Harissa

Make this soup and the harissa the day before to guarantee maximum flavour.

1 Preheat the oven to 200°C/400°F/Gas Mark 6. Prick the aubergines, place on a baking sheet and bake for 1 hour. When cool, peel and chop.

2 Heat the oil in a saucepan. Add the lamb and cook until browned. Add the onion, stock and water. Bring to the boil. Reduce the heat and simmer for 1 hour.

3 For the harissa, process the peppers, coriander seeds, chillies, garlic and caraway seeds in a food processor. With the motor running, add enough oil to make a paste. Season, then spoon into a jar. Cover with oil, seal and chill.

4 Remove the shanks from the stock, cut off the meat and chop. Add the sweet potato, cinnamon and cumin to the stock, bring to the boil, cover and simmer for 20 minutes. Discard the cinnamon and process the mixture in a food processor with the aubergine. Return to the saucepan, add the lamb and coriander and heat until hot. Serve with the harissa.

SERVES 6

PREPARATION TIME: 30 MINUTES, PLUS 30 MINUTES COOLING

COOKING TIME: 1 1/2 HOURS

2 aubergines

3 tbsp olive oil

6 lamb shanks

1 small onion, chopped

400 ml/14 fl oz chicken stock

2 litres/3 1/2 pints water

400 g/14 oz sweet potato, cut into chunks

5-cm/2-inch piece cinnamon stick

1 tsp ground cumin

2 tbsp chopped fresh coriander

For the harissa

2 red peppers, roasted, peeled, deseeded and chopped

1/2 tsp coriander seeds, dry-fried

25 g/1 oz fresh red chillies, chopped

2 garlic cloves, chopped

2 tsp caraway seeds

olive oil

salt

Sweetcorn & Smoked Chilli Soup

For this delicious soup, you can use fresh jalapeño chillies instead of the smoked version known as chipotle chillies if you prefer.

1 Heat the oil in a large, heavy-based saucepan. Add the onions and cook over a low heat, stirring occasionally, for 5 minutes, or until softened. Stir in the sweetcorn, cover and cook for a further 3 minutes.

2 Add the stock, half the milk, the chillies and garlic and season with salt. Bring to the boil, reduce the heat, then cover and simmer for 15–20 minutes.

3 Stir in the remaining milk. Reserve about 175 ml/ 6 fl oz of the soup solids, draining off as much liquid as possible. Transfer the remaining soup to a food processor or blender and process to a coarse purée.

4 Return the soup to the saucepan and stir in the reserved soup solids, the chorizo, lime juice and coriander. Re-heat to simmering point, stirring constantly. Ladle into warmed bowls and serve immediately.

SERVES 6

PREPARATION TIME: 20 MINUTES
COOKING TIME: 30–35 MINUTES

1 tbsp corn oil

2 onions, chopped

550 g/1 lb 4 oz frozen sweetcorn kernels, thawed

600 ml/1 pint chicken stock

425 ml/15 fl oz milk

4 chipotle chillies, deseeded and finely chopped

2 garlic cloves, finely chopped

salt

55 g/2 oz thinly sliced chorizo sausage

2 tbsp lime juice

2 tbsp chopped fresh coriander

Chilli con Carne

Forget the sloppy imitations of this Tex-Mex speciality – this is the real thing.

1 Heat half of the oil in a heavy-based saucepan. Add half the chopped onion and the garlic and cook, stirring occasionally, for 5 minutes, until softened. Remove with a slotted spoon.

2 Place the flour on a plate and season, then toss the meat in the flour to coat. Cook the meat, in batches, until browned all over, then return the meat and onion to the saucepan. Pour in the stock and wine and bring to the boil, stirring. Reduce the heat and simmer for 1 hour.

3 Meanwhile, heat the remaining oil in a frying pan. Add the remaining onion and the red chillies and cook, stirring occasionally, for 5 minutes. Add the beans and tomatoes with their juice and break up with a wooden spoon. Simmer for 25 minutes, until thickened.

4 Divide the meat between individual plates, top with the bean mixture and sprinkle with the green chillies. Serve with tortilla chips.

SERVES 6

PREPARATION TIME: 20 MINUTES

COOKING TIME: 1 1/2 HOURS

4 tbsp corn oil

2 onions, chopped

1 garlic clove, chopped

1 tbsp plain flour

salt and pepper

900 g/2 lb braising steak, diced

300 ml/10 fl oz beef stock

300 ml/10 fl oz red wine

2–3 fresh red chillies, deseeded and chopped

800 g/1 lb 12 oz canned red kidney beans, drained and rinsed

400 g/14 oz canned tomatoes

1 fresh green chilli, deseeded and sliced, to garnish

tortilla chips, to serve

Griddled Steak with Hot Chilli Salsa

SERVES 4

PREPARATION TIME: 15 MINUTES

COOKING TIME: 10–15 MINUTES

4 sirloin steaks, about 225 g/8 oz each

sunflower oil, for brushing

salt and pepper

For the salsa

4 fresh red habanero or Scotch bonnet chillies

4 fresh green poblano chillies

3 tomatoes, peeled, deseeded and diced

2 tbsp chopped fresh coriander

1 tbsp red wine vinegar

2 tbsp olive oil

This is a great way to serve steak cooked on a barbecue or under the grill, and the salsa is superb with any meat.

1 First make the salsa. Preheat the grill. Arrange the chillies on a baking sheet and cook, turning frequently, until blackened and charred. Leave to cool, then rub off the skins with kitchen paper. Halve and deseed the chillies, then chop finely.

2 Mix the red and green chillies, tomatoes and coriander together in a bowl. Blend the vinegar and oil together in a jug, season with salt and pour over the salsa. Toss well, cover and chill in the refrigerator until required.

3 Season the steaks with salt and pepper. Brush a griddle pan lightly with oil and heat over a medium heat until hot. Cook the steaks for 2–4 minutes on each side, or until cooked to your liking. Serve immediately with the salsa.

Spicy Pork Kebabs with Hot Satay Sauce

SERVES 6

PREPARATION TIME: 20 MINUTES, PLUS
3 HOURS MARINATING

COOKING TIME: 20 MINUTES

3 fresh green chillies, deseeded and
    chopped

1 onion, sliced

4 garlic cloves, finely chopped

5-cm/2-inch piece cinnamon stick,
    broken

2 tsp ground cumin

2.5-cm/1-inch piece fresh root ginger,
    grated

2 bay leaves

grated rind and juice of 1 lime

900 g/2 lb pork fillet, cut into cubes

sunflower oil, for brushing

For the sauce

2 fresh red chillies, deseeded and
    chopped

55 g/2 oz unsalted dry-roasted peanuts,
    roughly chopped

1 lemon grass stalk, chopped

1 garlic clove, chopped

8 shallots, chopped

1 tbsp chopped fresh coriander

1 tbsp groundnut oil

225 ml/8 fl oz canned coconut milk

1 tsp dark soy sauce

1 tbsp Thai fish sauce

2 tsp muscovado sugar

*Serve these tasty skewers with a refreshing crisp salad
for a perfect summer meal.*

1 Mix the green chillies, onion, garlic, cinnamon, cumin,
ginger, bay leaves, lime rind and juice together in a
shallow dish. Add the pork, turn to coat, then cover
and leave to marinate in the refrigerator for 3 hours.

2 Preheat the grill or barbecue. To make the sauce,
pound the chillies, peanuts, lemon grass, garlic,
shallots and coriander in a bowl with a pestle to make
a paste. Heat the groundnut oil in a frying pan. Add
the paste and cook over a low heat until golden. Stir
in the remaining sauce ingredients and bring to the
boil. Cover and keep warm.

3 Drain the pork and thread it on to 12 metal or pre-
soaked wooden skewers. Brush with oil and cook
under the grill or over hot coals, turning frequently,
for 8–10 minutes, until cooked through and tender.
Serve immediately with the sauce.

Pork with Chillies & Garlic

SERVES 4

PREPARATION TIME: 15 MINUTES, PLUS
10 MINUTES MARINATING

COOKING TIME: 5–7 MINUTES

650 g/1 lb 7 oz fresh lean pork mince

1 tbsp Thai fish sauce

5 fresh red bird's eye chillies

3 garlic cloves

3 tbsp groundnut or sunflower oil

1 tbsp soft brown sugar

2 tbsp dark soy sauce

2 tbsp oyster sauce

1–2 tbsp chicken stock or water
(optional)

fresh Thai basil sprigs, to garnish

Bird's eye chillies are fiery, so if you prefer a milder flavour substitute another variety of red chilli.

1 Mix the pork and fish sauce together in a dish and leave to marinate for 10 minutes.

2 If you like, halve and deseed the chillies. Pound the chillies and garlic together in a mortar with a pestle to make a paste. Heat the oil in a preheated wok or heavy-based frying pan. Add the pork and chilli paste and stir-fry over a high heat for 2–3 minutes, or until the meat has browned.

3 Add the sugar, soy sauce and oyster sauce and cook, stirring constantly, for 3–4 minutes, or until the pork is cooked. If the mixture seems too dry or about to scorch, add the stock or water. Serve immediately, garnished with Thai basil.

Stir-fried Chicken with Chillies & Thai Herbs

Not only do chillies feature in this dish, they also take a starring role in the garnish – not for the faint-hearted.

1 Cut off and discard the woody top part of the lemon grass stalk, leaving about 13 cm/5 inches of the bulb end, then chop very finely. Heat the oil in a preheated wok or frying pan. Add the chopped chillies, lemon grass and garlic and stir-fry for 2–3 minutes, until lightly coloured.

2 Add the chicken and stir-fry for 5 minutes, or until light golden brown. Stir in the fish sauce, soy sauce and sugar and continue to stir-fry for a further 4–5 minutes, or until the chicken is cooked through.

3 Stir in the coriander and the leaves from 3 of the basil sprigs. Transfer to a warmed serving dish and garnish with the sliced chillies and remaining basil.

SERVES 4

PREPARATION TIME: 10 MINUTES
COOKING TIME: 15 MINUTES

1 lemon grass stalk

3 tbsp groundnut or sunflower oil

4 fresh red bird's eye chillies, deseeded and chopped

4 garlic cloves, finely chopped

500 g/1 lb 2 oz skinless boneless chicken breasts, cut into cubes

3 tbsp Thai fish sauce

1 tbsp dark soy sauce

1 tsp sugar

1 tbsp chopped fresh coriander

4 fresh Thai basil sprigs

3 fresh red bird's eye chillies, thinly sliced, to garnish

Chicken & Chilli Enchiladas

Corn tortillas are wrapped around a spicy filling and baked in a tasty sauce for a substantial meal.

1 Preheat the oven to 180°C/350°F/Gas Mark 4 and brush a large, ovenproof dish with oil. Place two-thirds of the chillies, the onion, garlic, coriander, lime juice, stock, tomatoes and sugar in a food processor and pulse to a purée. Scrape into a saucepan and simmer over a medium heat for 10 minutes, until thickened.

2 Mix the remaining chillies, the chicken, 55 g/2 oz of the cheese and the oregano together. Season with salt and stir in half the sauce.

3 Heat the tortillas in a dry, heavy-based frying pan or in the microwave according to the packet instructions. Divide the chicken mixture between them, spooning it along the centres, then roll up and place, seam-side down, in the dish.

4 Pour the remaining sauce over the enchiladas and sprinkle with the remaining cheese. Bake in the oven for 20 minutes and serve hot.

SERVES 4

PREPARATION TIME: 25 MINUTES

COOKING TIME: 30–35 MINUTES

corn oil, for brushing

5 fresh hot green chillies, such as jalapeño or serrano, deseeded and chopped

1 Spanish onion, chopped

2 garlic cloves, chopped

2 tbsp chopped fresh coriander

2 tbsp lime juice

125 ml/4 fl oz chicken stock

2 beef tomatoes, peeled, deseeded and chopped

pinch of sugar

350 g/12 oz cooked chicken, shredded

85 g/3 oz queso anejo or Cheddar cheese, grated

2 tsp chopped fresh oregano

salt

8 corn or flour tortillas

Indian Chilli Chicken

A mixture of fresh chillies and chilli powder makes this a very fiery dish — it's also packed with flavour.

1 Make a slit along the side of each chilli. Heat the oil in a large, heavy-based frying pan. Add the chillies and cook over a low heat, turning occasionally, for 4–5 minutes, or until beginning to colour. Remove with a slotted spoon and reserve until required.

2 Add the onions, chilli powder, ginger, garlic, cumin, curry leaves and a pinch of salt to the frying pan and stir-fry for 2–3 minutes. Add the chicken and continue to stir-fry for 8–10 minutes, or until tender and cooked through.

3 Stir in the chopped coriander and lime juice, return the chillies to the frying pan and add the tomatoes. Stir briefly, then serve immediately with naan bread or freshly cooked rice.

SERVES 4

PREPARATION TIME: 10 MINUTES
COOKING TIME: 15–20 MINUTES

6–8 large fresh red chillies

4 tbsp sunflower oil

2 onions, chopped

1 tsp chilli powder

1 tsp grated fresh root ginger

2 garlic cloves, finely chopped

$\frac{1}{2}$ tsp cumin seeds

2 curry leaves

salt

650 g/1 lb 7 oz skinless boneless chicken breasts, cut into cubes

2 tbsp chopped fresh coriander

1 tbsp lime juice

4 tomatoes, quartered

naan bread or freshly cooked rice, to serve

Thai Green Curry

You can make this fragrant dish with beef, prawns, monkfish or, as here, chicken. Store leftover curry paste in the refrigerator.

1 First make the curry paste. Deseed the chillies if you like and roughly chop. Place all the paste ingredients in a mortar and pound with a pestle. Alternatively, process in a food processor. Gradually blend in the oil.

2 Heat 2 tablespoons oil in a preheated wok or large, heavy-based frying pan. Add 2 tablespoons of the curry paste and stir-fry briefly until all the aromas are released.

3 Add the chicken, lime leaves and lemon grass and stir-fry for 3–4 minutes, until the meat is beginning to colour. Add the coconut milk and aubergines and simmer gently for 8–10 minutes, or until tender.

4 Stir in the fish sauce and serve immediately, garnished with Thai basil sprigs and lime leaves.

SERVES 4

PREPARATION TIME: 25 MINUTES
COOKING TIME: 15–20 MINUTES

2 tbsp groundnut or sunflower oil

500 g/1 lb 2 oz skinless boneless chicken breasts, cut into cubes

2 kaffir lime leaves, roughly torn

1 lemon grass stalk, finely chopped

225 ml/8 fl oz canned coconut milk

16 baby aubergines, halved

2 tbsp Thai fish sauce

For the green curry paste

16 fresh green chillies

2 shallots, sliced

4 kaffir lime leaves

1 lemon grass stalk, chopped

2 garlic cloves, chopped

1 tsp cumin seeds

1 tsp coriander seeds

1 tbsp grated fresh root ginger or galangal

1 tsp grated lime rind

5 black peppercorns

1 tbsp sugar

salt

2 tbsp groundnut or sunflower oil

To garnish

fresh Thai basil sprigs

kaffir lime leaves, thinly sliced

Indonesian Chilli Prawns

This is a great dish for informal entertaining, as it tastes special but is very quick to prepare.

1 Using a sharp knife, finely chop the root ginger. Peel and devein the prawns.

2 Heat the oil in a preheated wok or large, heavy-based frying pan. Add the ginger, garlic, shallots, and chillies and stir-fry over a medium heat for 4–5 minutes, until the shallots are beginning to soften. Add the prawns and stir-fry for a further 3–5 minutes, or until the prawns have changed colour.

3 Add the coconut milk and stir in the ground and chopped coriander. Season to taste with salt and bring to the boil. Reduce the heat and simmer gently for 5 minutes, or until heated through.

4 Serve the chilli prawns immediately with freshly cooked rice.

SERVES 4

PREPARATION TIME: 10 MINUTES
COOKING TIME: 15 MINUTES

2.5-cm/1-inch piece fresh root ginger or galangal
500 g/1 lb 2 oz large raw prawns
2 tbsp groundnut or sunflower oil
2 garlic cloves, finely chopped
4 shallots, finely chopped
3 fresh red chillies, deseeded and thinly sliced
150 ml/5 fl oz canned coconut milk
1 tsp ground coriander
1 tbsp chopped fresh coriander
salt
freshly cooked rice, to serve

Chilli Crab

SERVES 4

PREPARATION TIME: 25 MINUTES

COOKING TIME: 10 MINUTES

2 cooked crabs, about 900 g/2 lb each

4 garlic cloves, chopped

2.5-cm/1-inch piece fresh root ginger, chopped

3 fresh red chillies, deseeded and chopped

4 tbsp groundnut or sunflower oil

4 tbsp tomato ketchup

2 tbsp dark soy sauce

1 tbsp dark brown sugar

150 ml/5 fl oz water

chopped spring onions, to garnish

Serve this fabulous dish in a large bowl and let everybody help themselves and eat the scrumptious morsels with their fingers.

1 Prepare each crab. Break off the claws, then turn the body on its back and push it out from the shell, using your thumbs. Remove and discard the stomach and 'dead man's fingers'. Chop the shell in half with a cleaver, cut the body section in half and crack the claws. Grind the garlic, ginger and chillies in a mortar with a pestle to make a paste.

2 Heat the oil in a preheated wok or large, heavy-based frying pan. Add all the crab pieces and stir-fry for 1 minute. Add the spice paste and stir-fry for a further 2 minutes.

3 Add the ketchup, soy sauce, sugar and water, stir well, then cover and simmer for 5 minutes. Transfer to a large serving bowl, garnish with the spring onions and serve immediately.

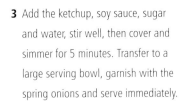

Fish with a Chilli Crust

SERVES 4

PREPARATION TIME: 15 MINUTES

COOKING TIME: 10 MINUTES

1 small bunch fresh coriander or
   flat-leaved parsley

3–4 dried red chillies, crushed

2 tbsp sesame seeds

salt and pepper

1 egg white

4 tuna steaks, about 140–175 g/
   5–6 oz each

2–3 tbsp sunflower oil

2 limes, halved, to garnish

This attractive and flavour-packed dish can be made with any firm-fleshed fish, such as cod or monkfish.

1 Chop the coriander or parsley leaving a few leaves whole to garnish. Mix the crushed chillies, chopped coriander or parsley and sesame seeds together in a shallow dish and season to taste with salt and pepper. Lightly beat the egg white with a fork in a separate shallow dish.

2 Dip the tuna steaks first in the egg white, then in the chilli and herb mixture to coat. Gently pat the crust evenly over the fish with the palm of your hand, making sure that both sides of the steaks are well covered.

3 Heat the oil in a large, heavy-based frying pan. Add the steaks and cook over a medium heat for 4 minutes, then turn them over carefully, using a fish slice. Cook for a further 4 minutes, then transfer to warmed serving plates. Garnish with the lime and the remaining coriander or parsley, and serve immediately.

Hot Potato Patties

This is a wonderful way to spice up potatoes and, if you cook and mash them in advance, is very quick.

1 Cook the potatoes in a large saucepan of lightly salted boiling water for 20–25 minutes, or until tender. Drain well and mash with a fork or potato masher. Tip into a bowl and leave until cool enough to handle.

2 Stir the chillies, almonds, coconut, coriander, flour and ginger into the mashed potato, mixing well, and season to taste with salt. Shape the mixture into small balls between the palms of your hands and gently flatten into patties.

3 Heat the oil for deep-frying to 180–190°C/350–375°F, or until a cube of bread dropped in the oil browns in 30 seconds. Fry the patties, in batches if necessary, for 5 minutes, or until golden. Drain on kitchen paper and serve immediately with the chutney.

SERVES 4

PREPARATION TIME: 20 MINUTES, PLUS
30 MINUTES COOLING

COOKING TIME: 30–40 MINUTES

500 g/1 lb 2 oz potatoes, peeled and
   cut into chunks

salt

2 fresh green chillies, deseeded and
   finely chopped

1 fresh red chilli, deseeded and finely
   chopped

1 tbsp blanched almonds, finely
   chopped

2 tbsp desiccated coconut

1 tbsp chopped fresh coriander or
   parsley

2 tbsp plain flour

2.5-cm/1-inch piece fresh root ginger,
   grated or very finely chopped

vegetable oil, for deep-frying

mango chutney, to serve

Tapas Potatoes with Chillies

SERVES 4–6

PREPARATION TIME: 10 MINUTES
COOKING TIME: 35–40 MINUTES

1 kg/2 lb 4 oz small new potatoes,
    unpeeled
salt and pepper
3 dried red chillies
4 tbsp olive oil
2 garlic cloves, finely chopped
4 spring onions, chopped
200 g/7 oz canned tomatoes
1 tbsp passata
1 tbsp sherry vinegar
$^{1}/_{2}$ tsp saffron threads, crushed

*Serve these potatoes as an accompaniment to a main course,
or pass a dish of them around with cocktail sticks for a Spanish-
style appetizer. They are delicious with a glass of chilled wine.*

1 Cook the potatoes in a large saucepan of lightly salted
boiling water for 10–15 minutes, or until only just tender.
Drain and leave until cool enough to handle.

2 Meanwhile, crush the chillies in a mortar with a pestle. Heat
the oil in a heavy-based saucepan. Add the garlic and spring
onions and cook over a medium heat for 5 minutes, until
softened. Stir in the crushed chillies, tomatoes with their juices,
passata, sherry vinegar and saffron and season to taste with
salt and pepper. Reduce the heat and simmer gently, stirring
occasionally, for 10 minutes.

3 Cut the potatoes in half and add to the saucepan, stirring
well to coat. Cover and simmer gently for a further
10 minutes. Taste, adjust the seasoning and serve hot
or at room temperature.

Singapore Noodles

This ever-popular dish is very versatile and, if you like, you can add prawns or strips of chicken to make it even more substantial.

1 Soak the noodles in a bowl of boiling water for 10 minutes, or according to the packet instructions. Meanwhile, drain the mushrooms, discard the stalks and slice the caps. Drain the noodles and pat dry with kitchen paper.

2 Heat half the oil in a preheated wok or frying pan. Add the noodles and a pinch of salt and stir-fry for 2 minutes. Transfer to a dish and keep warm.

3 Heat the remaining oil in the wok. Add the shallots, garlic and chillies and stir-fry for 2–3 minutes. Stir in the curry powder and cook, stirring, for 1 minute. Add the corn cobs, mangetout, green pepper and Chinese leaves and stir-fry for 5 minutes, or until the vegetables are tender but still have some 'bite'.

4 Stir in the mushrooms and return the noodles to the wok. Stir-fry for 2 minutes, then add the soy sauce. Serve immediately.

SERVES 4

PREPARATION TIME: 15 MINUTES, PLUS 30 MINUTES SOAKING

COOKING TIME: 12 MINUTES

225 g/8 oz rice noodles

25 g/1 oz dried Chinese mushrooms, soaked in hot water for 30 minutes

4 tbsp groundnut or sunflower oil

salt

4 shallots, chopped

2 garlic cloves, finely chopped

2 fresh green chillies, deseeded and finely chopped

2 tsp curry powder

115 g/4 oz baby corn cobs, halved

115 g/4 oz mangetout

1 green pepper, deseeded and sliced

115 g/4 oz Chinese leaves, shredded

2 tbsp soy sauce

Chilli Beans

Known as frijoles in Mexico, this dish is traditionally made with black haricot beans, but other types of bean may also be used.

1 Drain the beans, rinse well and place in a large, heavy-based saucepan. Cover the beans with cold water, then add the bay leaf, half the chopped onion, half the chopped garlic and the chillies. Bring to the boil and boil rapidly for 15 minutes. Reduce the heat, cover and simmer for 1 hour, adding more boiling water if necessary. Add 1 tablespoon of the oil and simmer for 30–45 minutes, until tender. Season with salt and reserve.

2 Heat the remaining oil in a frying pan. Add the remaining onion and garlic and cook, stirring occasionally, for 5 minutes, until softened. Add the tomatoes and cook for a further 5 minutes.

3 Add 3 tablespoons of the cooked beans to the frying pan and mash the mixture thoroughly. Stir the mixture into the remaining beans and re-heat gently. Taste and adjust the seasoning, if necessary. You can turn this dish into a hearty meal by serving with grated mozzarella cheese, baby tomatoes, spring onions and flour tortillas.

SERVES 6

PREPARATION TIME: 15 MINUTES, PLUS 3–4 HOURS SOAKING

COOKING TIME: 1–1 1/4 HOURS

350 g/12 oz dried black haricot or red kidney beans, soaked for 3–4 hours

1 bay leaf

2 onions, chopped

2 garlic cloves, finely chopped

2–3 fresh green chillies

2 tbsp corn oil

salt

3 tomatoes, peeled, deseeded and chopped

To garnish

mozzarella cheese, grated

baby tomatoes

spring onion

flour tortillas

Chilli Vodka

SERVES 2

PREPARATION TIME: 5 MINUTES, PLUS
1 HOUR STEEPING (OPTIONAL)

COOKING TIME: NONE

175 ml/6 fl oz chilli-flavoured vodka

2 pickled jalapeño chillies

ice cubes

dry vermouth, to taste

To prepare your own chilli vodka, steep fresh chillies in a bottle of vodka for several days, then strain and bottle once more.

1 Pour the vodka into a small jug. Deseed the chillies, if you like, then cut 2 large slices and reserve for decoration. Add the remaining chillies to the vodka, cover with clingfilm and place in the freezer for 1 hour. This makes the chilli flavour more pronounced, but this step may be omitted.

2 Wrap the ice cubes in a tea towel and hit with a meat mallet or rolling pin to break them up. Place the cracked ice in a mixing glass or jug. Pour in the vodka, add 2 dashes of vermouth for a very dry martini, or more if you prefer, and stir well until the outside of the glass is lightly frosted.

3 Strain the cocktail into 2 cocktail glasses, garnish with the reserved slices of chilli and serve immediately. Tortilla chips make a great accompaniment to this exotic cocktail.

Index